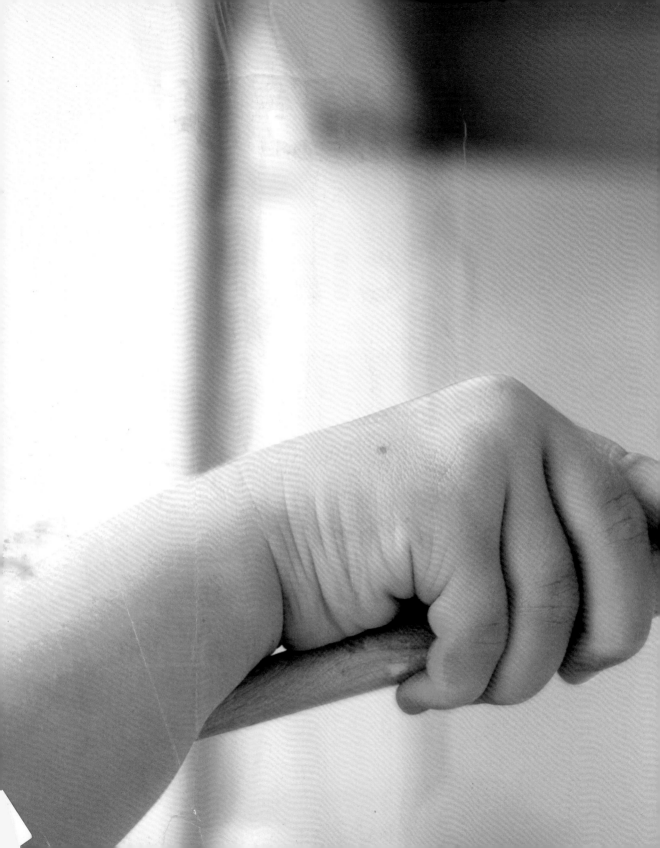

1 3 5 7 9 10 8 6 4 2

Published in 2014 by Vermilion, an imprint of Ebury Publishing
Ebury Publishing is a Random House Group company

FSC
www.fsc.org

MIX
Paper from
responsible sources
FSC® C104723

Designed and set by Ruth Mitchener
Photography by Ruth Mitchener

Printed and bound in China by Toppan Leefung

ISBN 9780091955151

Copies are available at special rates for bulk order. Contact the sales development
team on 02078408487 for more information.

To buy books by your favourite authors and register for offers
visit www.randomhouse.co.uk

RECIPES for PLAY

Fun activities for small hands and big imaginations

Recipes by Rachel Sumner
Photography by Ruth Mitchener

✔ermilion

CONTENTS

For Family
-R.M

TO MY CHILDREN,
THE BEGINNING OF
EVERYTHING CAME
WITH THE BEGINNING
OF YOU

- R.S

Dear Mess,

Why are we not better friends? I'm so
sorry. Considering you are the one who
never lets me down, who never fails me,
and whose company I can always rely
on, it seems odd that our relationship
isn't better. Why am I so affectionate
towards Clean and Tidy when they so
rarely visit? Why do I love Clean and
Tidy that much more when they are so
fleeting in their appearances?

It's time for a change. I would like to
welcome you into my home, dearest Mess.
I will attempt to mutter your name
under my breath no longer. So let's
make a deal. If we enjoy each other a
little more openly, perhaps you will be
more willing to leave when your welcome
has been outstayed? Sounds like a plan,
right?

Looking forward to a more open future
with you.

Warm regards,

The Parent

INTRODUCTION

Creative play provides the foundations that learning is built on. While great joy comes from play, great learning comes, too.

Recipes for Play helps you create opportunities for learning and exploration. Sensory play is important for all toddlers and pre-schoolers – they are natural-born scientists, hard-wired to learn and develop. They want to know everything, all the time. Some days it is a never-ending barrage of questions about the minutiae of life. Channel that enthusiasm and embark on an investigation together. Ponder the results of actions as a team and fill them with a sense of wonder and accomplishment.

There is no substitute for real-life sensory experiences. For example, there is only so much a screen can tell you about a flower. Sure, television can show you a super-high-definition, highly saturated colourful image of a flower, but it can't tell a child what that flower smells like, and there isn't an app on the market that can show what a flower really feels like when you squish the petals in your hand after ripping each one off. And what happens when you put the whole flower in water with leaves and soil? What does that feel like? There can be a time and a place for screen time, but it should not take the place of real-life experience. And, while TV can sometimes be a welcome babysitter, there are other sitters just waiting to mind your kids. Playdough has an excellent reputation in child minding. Why not invite her over to look after the kids next time you need a minute to finish folding the laundry?

MEANINGFUL MESS

Mess? What mess? There are a hundred different ways to parent. Sometimes those differences can divide, but there is one thing that unites every parent: mess. We're all plagued by it. Relentlessly. Children are mess-making machines.

Before I had children, I thought mess was just something that parents reluctantly had to accept. I never for a second thought that mess could be something one would willingly encourage. But, truth be told, I have found that directing the mess into specific play can actually reduce the overall chaos throughout the house. The idea of wilfully adding more mess to your already bulging workload may seem insane, but what if providing kids with ways to indulge in all that wonderful mess could have beneficial effects, like calm and satisfied children at the end of the day? Taking that leap into messy play at home doesn't have to be scary and, with a little thoughtful planning, it doesn't have to ruin your carpet either. Yes, they still leave a small wake of miscellany behind them wherever they go – but, by focusing all that exploration in a positive way, the kids are left sated and content with just the regular haphazard disarray, rather than the search-and-destroy kind.

LEARNING THROUGH PLAY

Children learn through their five senses – it's how they explore and understand their world. Providing play that helps kids tune in to their sensory impulses can seem daunting, but with clear set-up and tidy-up times, and using easy-to-source materials and ingredients found in most store cupboards, inviting your child to engage and create can be a breeze. The result for you, the parent, of inviting a little mess into your home, is a child full of wonder, fully present and excited by play. Focus less on the mess and more on the special time of teaching and learning and enjoying your children because, if you're getting involved in the play with them, they will most certainly be enjoying you!

When it comes to learning, meaningful play isn't about the noisiest toy, or the newest technology, just as parenting is about so much more than simply providing a child with food and shelter. Play should have no purpose but the play itself. When setting up an invitation to explore, you do so knowing that the only end product is mess and joy. Your child will learn no matter what – they are children, it is what they do naturally – but it won't necessarily be the kind of learning outcome you expect or desire. Sometimes expectations can get in the way of learning because, if you're quantifying play or seeking learning outcomes, it's not play anymore; it's just academic achievement by stealth.

There is no one correct way to play and there are no 'right' outcomes being sought here. Let your child direct the play. Follow their lead and trust that they know what they are doing, or at least that they have a plan and understand which direction they want to go in. Just because their idea of watching paint drip onto the floor might not be your idea of what painting should be, doesn't make it the wrong way to paint. It makes it a different way to paint. They may well be discovering the intricacies of gravity. Rice play will encourage kids to explore the quantum mechanics of flow, while yoghurt games delve into viscosity and the intrigues of colour. But these are just a wonderful side effect of play, not ends in themselves. Science, maths, language – these are all understood and engaged with in an innate way, not one that will enable them to pass a test about particular colours or scientific concepts.

Above all, and most importantly, engaged children are happy, connected children. And happy children are a lot easier to parent!

11

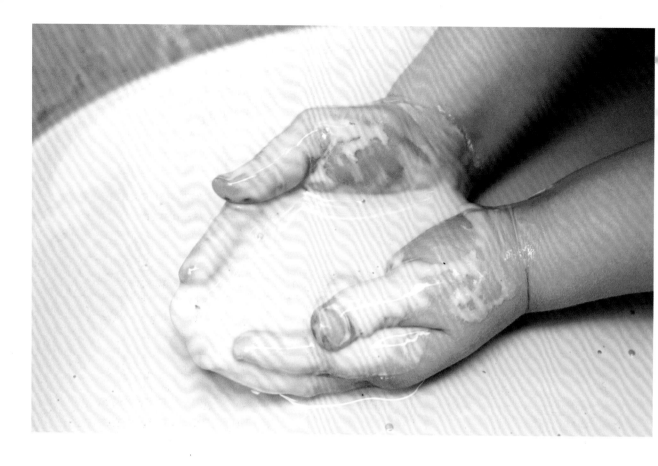

SENSORY GUIDE

While adults may understand that eating a crayon is not the wisest culinary choice, we probably figured this out by consuming one at some point.

Children can be told what is digestible and what is not, but nothing beats the full body experience to really understand.

Our senses are like a crude filing system of learning. Every new experience goes through a similar process: what does it smell, feel, taste, look or sound like? And from these simple beginnings come even more complex questions and answers. As we grow up these initial questions stay the same, but our filing abilities become so fast and effortless you don't even realise you're doing it.

Children are scientists from the very start; the world before them is a complex series of equations and investigations. When they try to lick your shoe, they aren't trying to annoy you and catch some unpleasant bug – they really just want to make sense of the funny thing on your foot. Play should be an open-door policy on sensory experiences. It should invite children to focus their senses productively. With our sensory guide you will be able to quickly reference which senses will be stimulated and engaged the most. Embrace the primitive sensory experience. Put your feet in the slime, too. Go on! See what it really feels like.

Throughout this book you will find these symbols indicating which of the five senses your child will engage with each recipe.

SEE

HEAR

TOUCH

SMELL

TASTE

GETTING STARTED

WHO THIS BOOK IS FOR

The recipes in this book promote free play, so children of all ages can enjoy taking it to their level of interest and ability. Although it is aimed at pre-schoolers, *Recipes for Play* is designed to be compatible with the differing interests and abilities of siblings and friends.

You know the abilities of your kids better than any book or guide. You will know if your baby is still in the 'putting everything in the mouth regardless of its edibility or safety' stage, and therefore will modify any play accordingly. And, while we're talking about knowing your baby best, remember that safety is up to you. Be especially careful with play that involves water and heights, and never leave your little ones unattended.

Play is definitely not limited to the younger members of your family, either, as many recipes can be enjoyable for everyone – even you! Just because you're an adult doesn't mean you're not allowed to also drop a great blob of paint from a height to see how gravity escorts it down. Being a grown-up is not your ticket out of free and easy fun. There is a time and a place for loopy adults, and children love nothing more than seeing you behaving like a fool and letting your hair down. The washing can always wait. The dishes aren't going anywhere. But your children are getting older.

MAKING YOUR OWN

Creating mess and opportunities for learning needn't be expensive, difficult or toxic. I bought face paint once, with the intention of letting my kids go to town on themselves and me. I remember the sharp chemical smell as I opened up the pots. I remember the cold, gluey texture. And I will always remember the colour, because I never did get the stain out of the chair cover that my daughter accidentally brushed past. Everything in my subconscious was yelling 'What on Earth is in this stuff?', but the kids were wide-eyed with anticipation and expectation, so I let it go. I later read about the high levels of lead in many children's face paints, and only then did I decide that there must be a better way. After an unsuccessful search for something safer, gentler and without the price tag of expensive adult make-up, I resigned myself to no more face painting. I just couldn't open those stinky pots again. But my girls kept asking me

for it.

Through sheer frustration (and after a lot of whining) I finally decided to see if I could make an alternative easily at home. It turns out that there is a lot you can achieve with cornflour and a little colour. And, really, who wants to be traipsing around from shop to shop, in and out of the car with small children, trying to find one ingredient to make something magical happen? Making sensory fun for pre-schoolers should be stress-free, easy and fun for you and your kids.

ALLERGY-FREE PLAY

Allergies shouldn't prevent children from enjoying messy play, so we have provided gluten-free options where possible. The majority of recipes are also dairy-free, but for the few that contain dairy products, we have indicated as such. If you do have a child with allergies, you will already be aware of the precautions you need to take; however, we always advise double-checking any packets of store-bought ingredients to make sure there are no hidden surprises.

CLEAN-UP

Young children learn by imitation and, whatever you are doing, they will want to copy. Embrace this enthusiasm and incorporate clean-up time into their play. Let them hold the mop or vacuum cleaner, or, after outdoor play on a warm day, have fun hosing down both play area and kids. Get them to pack toys away themselves. Tidying up not only encourages good habits, it also helps the development of fine motor skills in young children.

The clean-up in this book may vary from recipe to recipe, but there are many ways to make it easier – for instance, painting in the shower or covering the play area with newspaper or plastic sheeting.

Clean-up doesn't need to be toxic, either – white vinegar in water makes an excellent natural cleaning product, as does bicarbonate of soda. Sprinkle a little bicarbonate of soda on a damp cloth before wiping down surfaces. Or add some to a bucket of water for cleaning toys.

NATURAL COLOURS

It is possible to buy natural food colouring, but you can also make your own. It does require an outlay of time that many would probably rather use having a sit down and a cup of tea.

But it can also be really satisfying knowing that your kids are playing with 100 per cent natural products, made from scratch by you. Homemade colours will never work quite the same as their chemical cousins because they aren't as concentrated, so they create soft pastels rather than big bold hues.

Using homemade colours can be a more delicate equation than the store-bought versions because it takes a larger volume of colour to have the same effect as just a couple of drops of artificial colour. This means an increase in drying time, or using less water and more colouring when following recipes.

It is possible you will feel like a magazine-perfect homemaker, preparing a bounty of wholesome colour to freeze in ice trays and pop out when needed. If you're not freezing the colour, then it will need to be used within two weeks or discarded. It won't keep indefinitely the way artificial colour will.

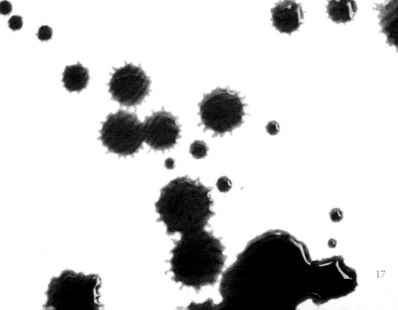

PURPLE	PINK	RED
Red cabbage leaves	**Blueberries**	**Beetroot**

Roughly chop the leaves of half a red cabbage, almost cover with water and boil for 15 minutes. Strain the water off the leaves using a colander and marvel at the beauty of the colour you have just created.

Frozen blueberries seem to yield the most colour; however, fresh are packed with a punch, too. Either machine-juice a handful of berries or do it the old-fashioned way and squeeze the beauty out of them through a muslin cloth.

Either juice the beetroot or use the same boil method used to make purple.

YELLOW/ORANGE
Turmeric powder

If a liquid is required, mix two teaspoons of turmeric powder with 225 ml (8 fl oz) of water in a small pot. Simmer for five minutes or so. Strain through a muslin cloth and cool.

GREEN
Dark leafy greens

Either throw them through the juicer (which will yield a more intense colour) or use the same boil method as purple. It is possible to get a bit cheeky when making the colour green and gather up all the wilting leafy greens in the back of the fridge to juice or simmer, and feel smug about your thriftiness.

BLUE
**Red cabbage &
bicarbonate of soda**

This is the hardest colour to reproduce naturally in the home kitchen, but possibly also the most fun. Boil chopped red cabbage following the purple recipe, then add bicarbonate of soda to the juice, a little at a time, to turn the liquid blue. As cool as this chemical reaction is to watch, it does create a volatile colour that is sensitive to heat and will react with vinegar.

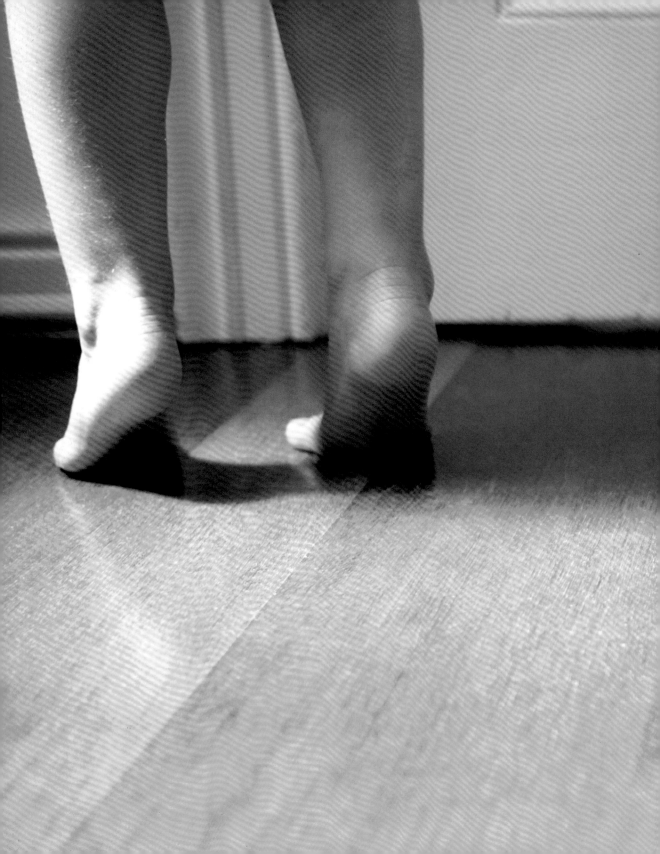

INDOOR PLAY

If your children are doing their job well, they will make sure they leave a little bit of themselves in each room of the house every day – a toy car here, a hair clip there, a nappy here, a puzzle piece there – until your whole house has become a shrine to infancy. While this may sound charming, it can be overwhelming. It might seem a bit crazy adding to this mess, but if you're cleaning up after them anyway, what's a little more? And, if it means you can get dinner on without the sweet harmony of crabby children at your feet, everyone will be a little happier.

Sometimes indoor play can give you a little breathing room, a quick cup of tea or a slice of toast. And sometimes it opens the door to a lot of family fun. You have permission to enjoy your children because they are enjoyable! And they aren't little for long. All too quickly they will be too cool for sofa play and colour droppers. Get in there while they still think you are superhuman!

YOGHURT PAINT

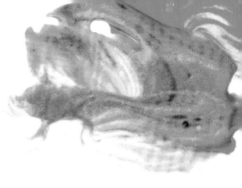

SET-UP TIME   short
CLEAN-UP TIME *moderate–long, depending on your set-up*
MESS FACTOR   *moderate*

There is a lot to love about yoghurt paint. It is perfect for the child who wants to put everything in the mouth and the parent who doesn't want the fear factor of giving young children real paint. It wipes clean easily, although, like most paints, it is not too friendly with carpets. If you're looking for a window of time to cook a meal, take your postcards off the fridge and let the kids paint the door.

YOU WILL NEED

plain Greek yoghurt
an ice cube tray or muffin tin
several different food
   colourings
brushes
paper (optional)

VEGAN ALTERNATIVE
Use plain soy yoghurt in place of Greek yoghurt.

Portion out the yoghurt into the ice cube tray or muffin tin. Mix in the food colouring to make a rainbow of 'paints'. Sit the little Picassos in front of the fridge or easel and marvel at their creativity. If you're concerned for the health of your fridge, magnet some paper to the surface.

This paint will dry and it is possible to keep the art for some time, provided the yoghurt isn't applied so thickly that it rots.

Both your fridge and the floor should wipe down quickly, or let the dog in and get it to do the work for you. If your darlings paint themselves more than the surface you've provided, you can always fill the kitchen sink, pop them in and get them to do the washing up while they're in there.

TEXTURE BALLOONS

SET-UP TIME   *long*
CLEAN-UP TIME *short*
MESS FACTOR   *low*

There can be more to balloons than just air. Filling them with different textured fillings and tying them off leaves you with curious malleable toys. Make pairs with the same fillings and ask the kids to match textures, or draw faces on the balloons with a marker and enjoy the change of expression with each squish.

Rummage through your cupboards for a selection of different fillings, such as flour, dried lentils, polenta or salt. Watch out for sharp or pointy grains that could pierce the balloons, such as rice or angular pasta.

YOU WILL NEED

balloons (helium-grade work best as they are stronger)
a funnel
various dry goods as filling

Some fancy finger-work may be required, as well as a bit of patience. Stretch the mouth of each balloon over your funnel and slowly feed the dry goods inside. This may involve some stretching and squeezing and wiggling of the balloon, or a sneaky prod with a chopstick to force reluctant filling into the vessel. If you're using flour, beware the squeeze as the flour is likely to leap right back out of the funnel and into your face, which can be amusing but also frustrating.

When tying off the end, slowly squeeze the air out before knotting the balloon. Alternatively, you can get really fancy and double back the balloon by twisting the neck a couple of times and folding it back over the body, then stretching another balloon over the top and repeating the twisting technique. It does offer a cleaner finish but, really, kids aren't that fussy, and if you're grumpy after getting a face full of flour, a basic knot will suffice.

TAPED UP

SET-UP TIME   *long, but it's half the fun*
CLEAN-UP TIME *short*
MESS FACTOR   *moderate*

When the weather is poor and the kids start to go a little stir-crazy indoors, it is possible to turn an entire room into a racetrack, or a zoo, or a great work of art! You are only limited by the amount of tape you have.

YOU WILL NEED

masking tape
mini toy cars, animal
   figurines or other toys
a rainy day

Because you're using masking tape, which does not have the same stick factor as other tapes, you're free to let your imagination run wild with this activity. Create roadways, enclosures or off-the-wall artistic designs. Use the tape like chalk to set up indoor games such as hopscotch. Trace around each other, measure your feet together or enjoy getting on the floor and creating something vast and impressive with the kids. Whole cities can be constructed. They can be as simple or as complex as you like. Go over the sofa, around the cat, under the coffee table. Erect bridges between items of furniture or go off-road with crazy gravity-defying streets.

When the kids have had enough, or the sun comes out, just peel back the tape to tidy up.

SALT DOUGH

SET-UP TIME   *short, but this activity can roll over a few days*
CLEAN-UP TIME *long*
MESS FACTOR   *moderate–high*

One of the best things about salt dough is the ability to insert your children at any point of the process. For some, decorating pre-cut baubles will be wonderfully engaging play; for others, the entire process of mixing, kneading, rolling and cutting will be much enjoyed. You will know what your children enjoy and are capable of.

Well-dried salt-dough ornaments can last for years and are perfect for festive decorations. Making or decorating ornaments every year can become a special family tradition.

YOU WILL NEED

280 g (10 oz) plain flour
350 g (12 oz) salt
1 tbsp vegetable oil
a good squeeze of lemon juice
225 ml (8 fl oz) lukewarm
    water
rolling pin
biscuit cutters
a straw or chopstick
greaseproof paper
paint, glue and items for
    decorating
ribbon

Mix the dry ingredients together. Add the vegetable oil and lemon juice to the water, then slowly add to the dry mixture, turning it into a soft dough. If it is too sticky, add more salt; if too gritty, add more flour.

Turn the dough out and knead it on a flat surface for a good 10 minutes. The more you work it, the softer it should become. Leave it to rest for 15 minutes before you roll it out.

Roll the dough flat on a floured surface, then using the biscuit cutters, cut to your heart's content. Try to discourage sly tasting (yes, it is disgusting, and no, it doesn't taste like uncooked shortbread).

Make a hole in each ornament as you go so the ribbon can be threaded through. A straw or chopstick is perfect for this. Your children can help make indentations and textures, or press in fake jewels or other visual delights. Lay the cut-out creations on greaseproof paper for drying.

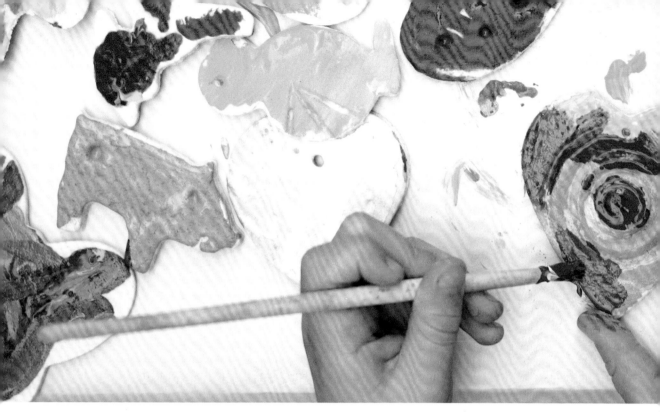

The dough shapes can be air-dried, which can take about 48 hours; or, they can be oven-dried, which will take about 4 hours. Use a cool oven (about 90°C/200°F). Getting enthusiastic and turning up the heat will not speed up the drying time – it will just give you cracked and bubbly dough. Drying time is an estimate. If you make a really creative 3D sculpture, expect it to take longer.

Once dry, get your children's decorating mojo flowing. Anything goes: they can paint, glue, add sparkle. Thread some ribbon and use these long-lasting treasures as decorations or gifts.

When they've finished, pull out the vacuum cleaner to pick up any stray dough or decorating debris. Unused dough can be stored in the fridge in an airtight container for up to a week.

GLUTEN-FREE!
Mix 125g (4½ oz) of cornflour with 560g (1¼ lb) of bicarbonate of soda and a little more than 225ml (8 fl oz) of water in a pot. On a low heat, stir until your arm hurts and the mixing spoon wants to break. Turn it out onto a lightly (corn)floured surface and wait for it to cool down. Cornflour gets very hot and holds the heat well, so be careful. Once cool, treat it the same as regular salt dough.

RAINBOW RICE

SET-UP TIME *moderate*
CLEAN-UP TIME *short*
MESS FACTOR *low—moderate, depending on how much your children like throwing stuff*

As far as messy play goes, this one is pretty clean, providing you use a sheet to play on. The tipping and pouring qualities of rice are similar to sand, without the microscopic grains going everywhere. Rice vacuums up quickly and easily, and the bright colours make it easy to spot.

If you make the rice in advance, the set-up is really fast. The hand sanitiser is used to adhere and distribute the colour. White vinegar is an excellent natural alternative, however this needs to dry overnight, while the sanitiser takes 15 minutes. As with the intensity of natural colour, the more vinegar used the easier it is to distribute the colour, but the longer the drying time.

YOU WILL NEED

rice – 1 kg (2 lb 4 oz) is a
  good place to start
plastic bags (make sure they
  don't have any holes)
hand sanitiser or white
  vinegar
food colouring
old newspaper
a large sheet suitable for
  playing on
tools for tipping and mixing,
  such as child-friendly pots,
  pans, mixing spoons, egg
  cups, bowls and beakers

Decide how many colours you want to make. Portion out your rice into plastic bags accordingly. For every handful of rice, add a good squirt of hand sanitiser, or about a teaspoon of vinegar, and either a few drops of artificial colouring or about a quarter of a teaspoon of natural colouring, depending on how bright you want the batch to be and how much drying time you have. Remember that natural colouring requires more volume than artificial to achieve similar results.

Squeeze out the air and close off each bag, then massage the colour through the rice. When you're satisfied with the evenness of colour distribution, pour the rice out onto a sheet of newspaper and leave to dry. Drying time depends on the distributor used.

When you have your stash of dry and colourful rainbow rice, lay out the big sheet, bring out some tools for tipping and mixing, and watch your children go to town.

When they're done with the mess, simply remove everything that isn't rice, collect the corners of the sheet and funnel your rice into a container ready to play with another day. Vacuum up any grains that escape the sheet, and no one will know – until you post the cute pictures on Facebook, of course.

POSTING BOX

SET-UP TIME *long*
CLEAN-UP TIME *short*
MESS FACTOR *low*

You can encourage quiet concentration with the help of a cardboard box and a handful of buttons. Sorting and posting are such simple joys that they are often overlooked. If the items for sorting get tiresome, the play can be easily revived with a switch of postal supplies: swap buttons for pompoms, coloured matchsticks or magnets. The style of sorting is limitless: they can sort colours, numbers, shapes or textures. Bigger items are easier and safer for the smaller hands.

YOU WILL NEED

a craft knife (for you, not the kids)
a shoe box is ideal but any small cardboard box will do
a marker and felt-tip pens
a selection of similar items to sort or post, such as buttons of different colours and sizes

Using the craft knife, cut a handful of holes in the lid of the box corresponding in size with the items you have for posting. Decorate the lid of the box to make it a little more enticing. The idea is to create a box that screams out, 'Post something in here!'

Leave the magical post box you have created somewhere for your child to discover, conveniently set up with posting items close at hand, and enjoy the peace that comes with the concentration of sorting and posting. It really is all about the simple pleasures when you're small.

Encourage your child to post all the objects back into the box at the end of play to make tidy-up a breeze!

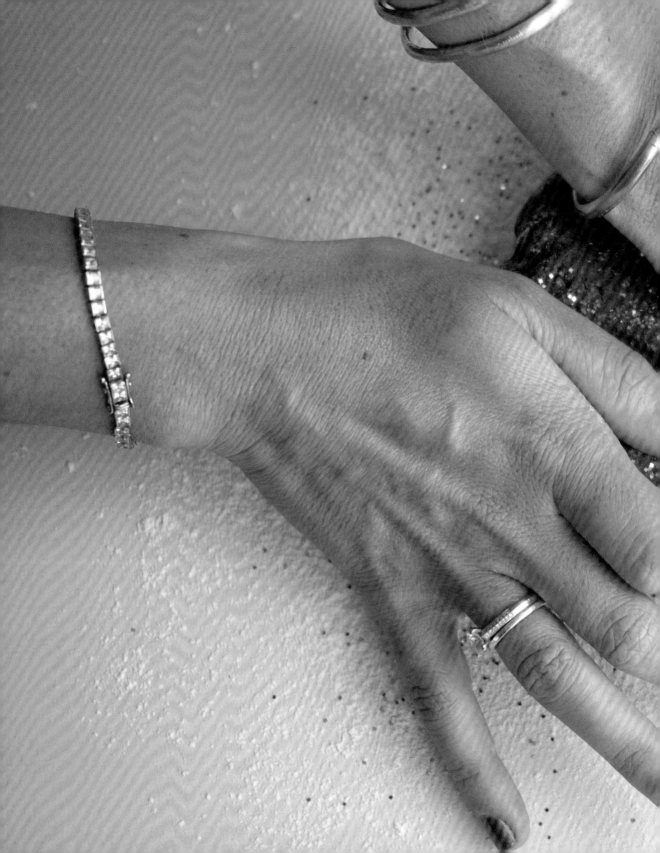

PLAYDOUGH PLUS

SET-UP TIME   *long*
CLEAN-UP TIME *moderate*
MESS FACTOR   *low*

Shop-bought playdough isn't a patch on the homemade stuff, especially when you can bump your dough to the next level with smell and sparkle (not to mention the added bonus of being all-natural and chemical-free). This is about the only time I would recommend using glitter in the home, as it is contained in the dough. Making your own dough is fast and easy and it will keep indefinitely, provided you store it in an airtight container or plastic bag and your kids don't mess it up too much.

YOU WILL NEED

140g (5 oz) plain flour
175g (6 oz) salt
225ml (8 fl oz) water
2 tsp cream of tartar
1 tbsp plain cooking oil
food colouring*
glitter
essential oils of your choice
tools for rolling/cutting/
  squashing (muffin cases are
  great fun, too)

GLUTEN-FREE!
Use 250g (9 oz) cornflour instead of regular flour and increase the oil to 125ml (4 fl oz). It does not mix like traditional dough, it holds the heat for a lot longer and the elasticity isn't as great, but allergies shouldn't hold kids back from play!

Add flour, salt, water, cream of tartar, oil and food colouring to a small pot and cook over a medium heat, stirring constantly. After a couple of minutes, you will notice the mixture clumping a bit. It will then start to get difficult to stir, eventually making a big lump.

Turn the lump out onto a floured bench and knead. Press it out into a dough pancake, shake glitter all over it, fold it in and knead it some more. Do the same with an essential oil, adding a few drops. Peppermint will add a lovely invigorating aroma or, for calming play, try lavender oil. If you're entertaining snotty kids at home, decongest them while they play with a bit of eucalyptus oil in their dough. If dough gets into the carpet, no need to fret; when it dries, it will vacuum right up.

* Note: if you're using homemade colours, they should be added as water replacement – so if you use 125ml (4 fl oz) colour, you then need only 125ml (4 fl oz) water.

Be careful if you use natural blue; cooked into playdough, it alters the consistency to a more foamy and ultimately brittle dough. It still makes a fun dough but it will turn to porridge-like sludge over a couple of days (science really is cool!).

PAPER-ROLL PLAY

SET-UP TIME *short*
CLEAN-UP TIME *short*
MESS FACTOR *low*

Drawing doesn't always have to be with a pen on paper. Much of what is discarded as waste is actually a lot of adventure waiting to happen. Cardboard paper rolls from kitchen paper and loo rolls are a prime example: before you throw out the recycling, get out the washable pens and start creating. Paper rolls can become anything from cats to owls, finger puppets to family figurines. While you're at it, save your egg cartons and boxes, too, at least until after you've let the children loose on them.

This activity is more suitable for the older pre-schooler, but all children's art is amazing and, if they can hold a pen, chances are they will create something marvellous.

YOU WILL NEED

cardboard paper rolls
washable pens or pencils
glue
feathers, tissue paper,
    pompoms, googly eyes,
    pipe cleaners, etc.
imagination

You are limited only by the interests of your children with this activity, because anything is possible with a cardboard paper roll and some creative supplies.

With some minor manipulation, it is possible to squash and fold one end of a paper roll to make ears, then leave the canvas free for animal interpretation: cats, squirrels, monkeys, penguins. Add googly eyes and pipe cleaners to open up the possibilities even further.

Try bending and creasing one end of a roll to make a simple stamp. Think heart shapes, stars or squares.

Use white vinegar in water to clean up any stray glue that finds its way on to your floor or furniture.

PAPIER MÂCHÉ

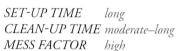

SET-UP TIME	*long*
CLEAN-UP TIME	*moderate–long*
MESS FACTOR	*high*

Play invitations do not need to involve expensive materials; papier mâché is proof of this. Papier mâché can be real project play, and is one of the few invitations where you may be left with an end product to further clutter your house.

While the possibilities for papier mâché are endless for the preschool-aged child, these instructions use balloons, bottles and muffin tins as moulds. Of course, if your little sculptor has big dreams, by all means create something epic! If the participants are quite young, it can be beneficial to provide a pile of pre-torn paper.

YOU WILL NEED

flour
water
olive oil
inflated balloons, bowls,
    empty plastic bottles,
    muffin tins
old newspaper torn into strips

Mix flour with water until you have a glue-like consistency. This is normally at quantities of about four parts flour to one part water. It should be noted that although this is just flour and water, it is an efficient adhesive, so wearing messy clothes is advised and newspaper should be laid down to protect surfaces.

Oil your item to mâché with the olive oil. This will provide a barrier between the base object and the mâché, so that when the creation dries it can be parted from its mould easily.

Coat strips of newspaper in the glue until they are soggy and let the children experiment with placing the paper on the mould. If you'd like a finished product from this play that you can take to the next step of decoration, you may need to sit down with them and make one too.

When they're satisfied with their creation, leave the sculpture to dry for at least 36 hours. You will see a change in the colour of the creation as the glue dries. Then either pop

the balloon or, if using another mould, gently pull the creation away.

You can squeeze even more mileage from this play by cracking out the paints and going to town decorating the dried sculpture.

Use hot water with a little white vinegar to clean up any glue that finds its way on to the floor or furniture.

GLUTEN-FREE!
Replace regular flour with cornflour and a teaspoon of either xanthan or guar gum. Add the cornflour and gum mixture a little at a time to warm water to avoid clumping. A ratio of 1:1 water to flour is about right but, as with regular papier mâché glue, it is more about texture and feel than exact quantities. You are going for a slimy and gloopy texture, not too watery and not too thick.

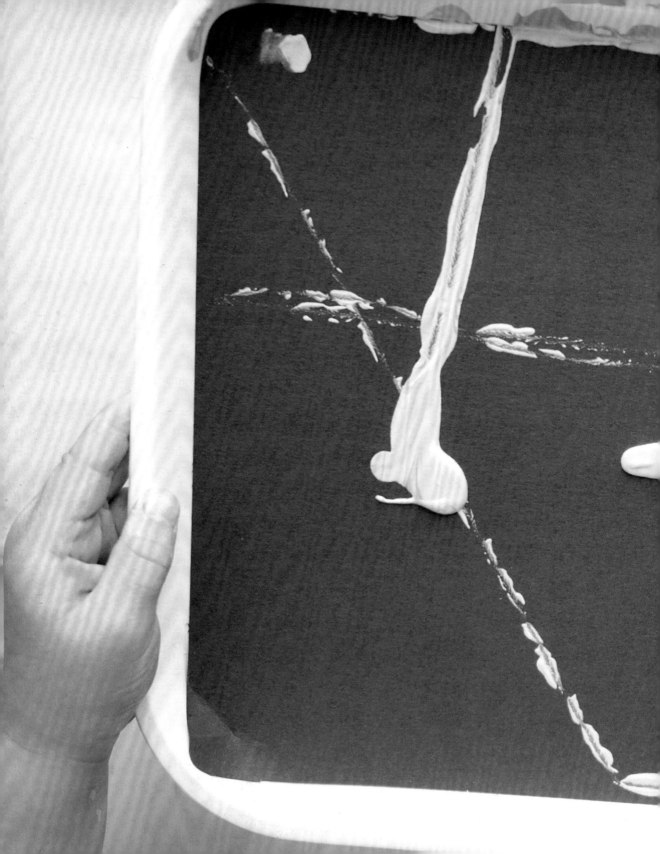

MARBLE PAINTING

SET-UP TIME *moderate*
CLEAN-UP TIME *moderate*
MESS FACTOR *moderate*

Making a mark is possible with all manner of tools, and marble painting is another expression of this. Rolling the marble over the tray takes practice and concentration but, by painting standards, it is fast, creative, exciting and well-contained. You can use a variety of dishes, from baking sheets to cake tins to foil roasting pans. The only requirements are that the sides are high enough so the marble doesn't jump out and that it is light enough for your child to manipulate it easily.

YOU WILL NEED

several colours of paint
small cups (one for each
  colour of paint)
marbles (one or two for each
  cup)
teaspoons (one for each cup)
plain paper
a shallow, contained dish

Put a little paint into the bottom of each cup (one colour per cup), then add a marble or two to each and a teaspoon to retrieve the marbles.

Cut the paper to fit into the bottom of the dish. Ask the children to fish the marbles out one at a time and place them on the paper. Get them to roll and rotate the dish to create patterns and designs on the paper.

Enjoy making a mess without the paint going all over your walls. Just beware the rogue slippery marble that tries to make a run for it across the floor and under the fridge! Using washable paints will make clean-up easy, as you can simply wash the dishes in the sink when you've finished.

JELLY EGGS

SET-UP TIME   *long*
CLEAN-UP TIME *short*
MESS FACTOR   *low*

There is nothing more fun than messing with a child's assumptions about life. Jelly eggs are the perfect example of this. They look like boiled eggs, they crack open like boiled eggs, but they most certainly are *not* boiled eggs.

If you're worried about certain ingredients in regular jelly, it's possible to source vegetarian, naturally coloured and allergy-friendly jelly.

It can be important to keep in mind the very low possibility of salmonella contamination from eggshell. We would always recommend washing the empty shell with hot water. Take your time. Eggshell is an amazing creation. It can be a good idea to have more shells than you need. Thoroughly cleaning something so strong and also so fragile can take a little practice.

YOU WILL NEED

whole eggshells
an empty egg carton
packet of jelly
opaque egg cups

Collect whole eggshells. You can do this over a couple of weeks: whenever an egg is required, instead of cracking it open, gently tap a hole in one end big enough to shake out the contents. Take care to wash the eggshells out well. Store them in the egg carton.

Once you have your collection of eggshells washed and dried, make up the jelly following the instructions on the packet. Do this at least the night before you want to serve the eggs, to give the jelly time to set.

Using the egg carton to hold the eggshells hole-side up, fill them with the warm liquid jelly. Place the carton in the fridge and allow the jelly to set.

When it is time to serve the eggs, place them hole-side down in the egg cups to hide the opening. Enjoy the discovery and confusion.

FIZZ DROPPERS

SET-UP TIME   *moderate*
CLEAN-UP TIME *long*
MESS FACTOR   *moderate*

Something amazing happens when you mix bicarbonate of soda with vinegar – something fizzy and volcanic! Add colour to the vinegar, make the bicarbonate of soda a canvas, and it's open season for scientific painting fun.

YOU WILL NEED

an ice cube tray, muffin tin or
   similar
white vinegar
several different food
   colourings*
bicarbonate of soda
a small shallow dish, such as a
   plastic takeaway container
a tea towel
eye droppers

Fill the ice cube tray or muffin tin with vinegar. Add several drops of food colouring to each compartment and mix well.

Sprinkle out an even layer of bicarbonate of soda in the dish – enough to cover the bottom. This will be the canvas. Use the tea towel as a placemat to stop anything slipping around and to catch any drips.

Children can use the eye droppers as paint brushes, the vinegar as paint and the bicarbonate of soda as a canvas. Enjoy volcanic results!

Clean-up is easy, as your volcano can be simply washed down the sink.

* Note: because you want the vinegar to react with the bicarbonate of soda, shop-bought food colouring tends to work best as it is more concentrated than natural alternatives, and you don't want the mighty power of the vinegar to be diluted.

SOFA PLAY

SET-UP TIME   *short*
CLEAN-UP TIME *short*
MESS FACTOR   *low*

Your sofa is so much more than just a place to park your bottom once the kids are asleep. It can be a wonderful tool for vibrant indoor physical play. When the weather is miserable and the kids are fizzing with energy, let it out on the sofa. Obviously, it is a wise idea to move aside any furniture that may be inclined to injure your children, such as sharp-cornered coffee tables or anything made of glass, and supervision is important. At the very least, encourage the big jumps while you sit back and watch with a cup of tea.

If you're also feeling energetic, this is a great opportunity to vacuum under the sofa cushions and give them a little fluff up while you're there. If you're light on padding, you can raid the bedrooms for pillows, blankets, quilts and duvets.

YOU WILL NEED

cushions – lots of them
a sofa
a sheet
laundry pegs (optional)

Option 1: The Billy Goat Tower
Pile high as many cushions as you have available, making a mountain as tall as possible. Challenge your children to make like mountain goats and reach the top.

Option 2: The Housing Experiment
With the addition of a sheet, an impressive fort can be erected for camping, or castle wars, or pirate battles, or a vet clinic, or a fairy nook. Laundry pegs can come in handy when attempting to make your walls and ceilings stick to the sofa base.

Option 3: Flumping
Pull all available cushions off the sofa and pile at the foot or side (depending on age and physical ability) of the sofa. Treat it like a ball pit. Children can roll and jump off the couch. You can construct slides using firmer cushions or rolling runways by laying out all the cushions in a line.

COLOUR MIXING

SET-UP TIME   moderate
CLEAN-UP TIME moderate–long
MESS FACTOR   moderate

This is an activity that requires calm and concentration. Don't do it when your children are bursting at the seams to get out and do something physical and adventurous! This is a great parallel-play set-up, meaning that two or more children can play together without interacting, so it has the potential to be peaceful and calm.

YOU WILL NEED

an ice cube tray
water
several different food
   colourings
paper towels or tissues
eye droppers

Fill half the compartments of the ice cube tray with water and add a few drops of food colouring to each. If you're using homemade colour, you won't need to water it down: just add it straight. Vary the shades and intensity. If you want to open up conversation about colour development, only use the primary colours (red, yellow and blue) to show how all other colours are derived from these three.

Children can mix the colours together in the ice cube tray or drip them on to the paper towels or tissues to create something more tangible (eye droppers are great for little hands just honing their fine motor skills).

You can also turn this art into a kind of stained-glass window by sticking the paper towels or tissues on a window. If wet enough, the creations will adhere themselves without any fuss. Children feel proud seeing a whole window turned over to their art. When you're ready to take your windows back, simply open the doors and let a gust of wind 'accidentally' brush them off.

Use warm water with a little white vinegar to clean up any spillages.

COLLAGE

SET-UP TIME   *moderate (the time is taken collecting supplies)*
CLEAN-UP TIME *moderate*
MESS FACTOR   *moderate*

The idea is a simple one: take paper, glue and objects of interest. Mix well. With a variety of trinkets and textures, some incredible discoveries can take place. Finding well-contained glue is the only real challenge here. Pots with brushes are great at minimising the mess, as are glue sticks and wands.

Beware of glitter. It looks pretty, but you will continue to find it all over the floor for weeks to come, no matter what kind of floor covering you have. The same can be said for sand: there is nothing worse than sand in the bed, yet somehow it always finds its way there. If you're after a little sparkle without the contagious effect of glitter, make your own coloured Epsom salts by rubbing a little food colouring through a small bagged portion of the salts and drying them on a sheet of newspaper.

YOU WILL NEED

supplies for gluing (we enjoy
   coloured Epsom salts,
   dried lentils, pasta shapes,
   polenta, fabric scraps,
   feathers, seeds, dried leaves
   – anything goes!)
old newspaper or similar
paper
glue
ice cube tray or muffin tin
a damp cloth for sticky hands

Choose a range of supplies for gluing. Having large quantities of items is less important than having variety.

Cover your work surface with the newspaper, then set out the paper, glue and collage supplies – ice cube trays and mini muffin tins are great for this. Enjoy the amazing art that pours forth.

Find a clear, flat surface to dry all the creations on, then post them off to unsuspecting relatives.

Involve the little artists in vacuuming up any stray debris, and make clean-up part of the fun.

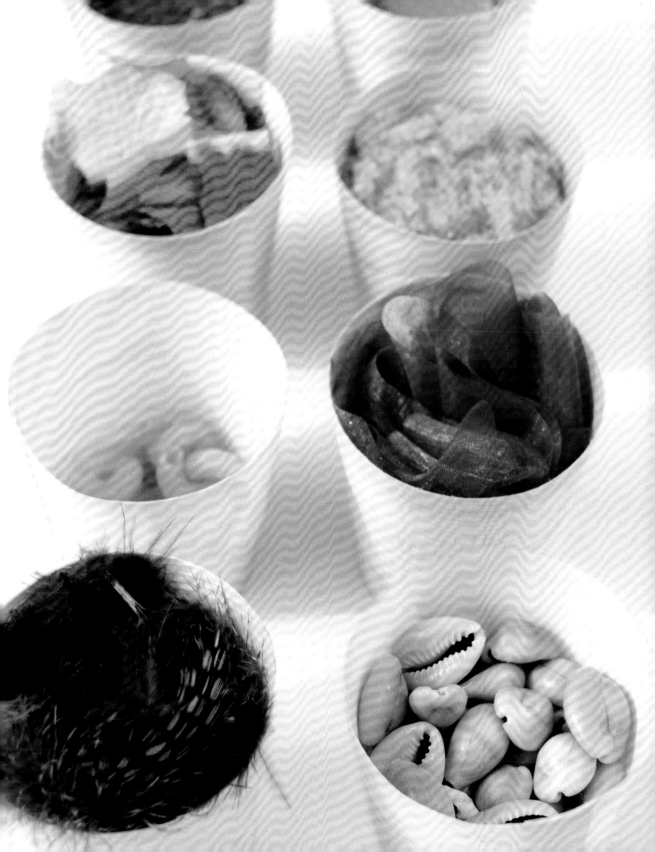

BATHROOM REDECORATION

SET-UP TIME   short
CLEAN-UP TIME moderate
MESS FACTOR   moderate

If they're itching for a little creativity, but the idea of cleaning up after Picasso leaves you tired before you've even started, then consider the sanctuary that is your bathroom. Provided you're using washable painting materials, you can contain your artists, and your sanity, by getting them to decorate the inside of your bath or shower – because when they're done, they can wash off and clean up all at the same time.

YOU WILL NEED

a muffin tin or egg carton
shaving foam* (probably
   a good idea not to use
   Daddy's finest)
several different food
   colourings
a chopstick or similar
brushes
a shower or bath

Fill the compartments of the muffin tin or egg carton with the shaving foam. Put a couple of drops of food colouring on to each 'fluffy cloud mountain' and mix well with the chopstick.

Get your artists naked or in clothing that you don't mind getting really messy and/or wet. Set them to task decorating the inside of the bath or shower. Take some pictures – you will want to remember the day your bathroom turned into a paint-astic bombsite. Ask the children if it is possible for them to paint the entire bath. It just might be.

Because you're working with a wet-friendly surface, when their work is done, all you need to do is turn the shower on and clean both children and bathroom. If you're quick, you might even squeeze in a sneaky hair wash before they catch wind of what you're up to.

* Note: if you don't have any shaving foam, it is possible to use poster paint for this play; just make sure it is washable so that it will clean off easily and won't stain your bath.

OUTDOOR PLAY

Children love being outdoors. Luckily for you, not only is it easier to clean up after kids when the mess is outdoors (hose it all down!), but the fresh air and sunshine are also good for them. If the weather is less than ideal, outdoor play is still possible with sufficient wet-weather gear and a toasty warm jumper.

If you're light on garden space, take over your local park. Pack a snack and settle in; just be sure to take everything home when you're done. Don't forget your essentials either: a good hat, the right clothes for the weather and supervisory eyes around water. Like the adventurer Sir Ranulph Fiennes famously said, 'There is no bad weather, only inappropriate clothing.'

WINDOW DRESSING

SET-UP TIME short
CLEAN-UP TIME long
MESS FACTOR moderate

If you have a painting enthusiast who just can't seem to stick to the paper, then window painting is a glorious alternative. Provided the paint you're using is washable (just because all paint for children should be, that doesn't mean it is), then there is little harm that can't be remedied with a good hose and a window squeegee, which is also a lot of fun when you're small.

YOU WILL NEED

a decent-sized window at
    child-friendly height
washable paints, in pots or a
    muffin tin
paint brushes
paint-friendly clothes for your
    artist
a hose and squeegee for clean
    up

If you're concerned about your decking or paving getting dripped on, then an old dust sheet is a great precaution, because the less time you spend hovering and stressing, the better for everyone. Children should be able to paint with free abandon as much as possible.

Lay out the paints, point your child in the direction of the approved painting surface and let them go to town. The great thing about this play is that you can watch them from the other side of the glass and make silly faces at them while they paint, or push your face against the glass and get them to paint you through the window.

When it is time to clean up, crank out the hose and squeegee and enjoy a whole new round of play. It can be a lot of fun for the children to be on one side of the glass and a parent on the other, 'getting them' with a hose.

TOUCH TUB

SET-UP TIME   *long initially, short after the first time*
CLEAN-UP TIME *short–moderate*
MESS FACTOR   *low–moderate*

Do you ever have to fight the urge to push your whole hand into bulk grain bins at the shops, just to see how it feels? Do you find yourself compelled to dig your toes into the sand when you're at the beach? Go on, admit it, you still love a sensory experience! Don't deny yourself any longer. Get a sensory touch tub for the garden. It is so easy to set up, you can change the sensory experience with little fuss and you, too, can put your whole hand in a bucket full of grains.

YOU WILL NEED

a shallow tub, preferably with
   a lid for future storage
something tactile to fill it
   with
toys to experience the
   sensation with

Under-the-bed storage containers are ideal for this because you can just roll the tub away when you're done for the day and, provided your angel hasn't flung the contents far and wide, that's a pretty quick clean-up.

Fill your tub with your tactile environment. Think along the lines of:
- dried lentils
- rice
- whole popcorn kernels
- wheat
- sand (you brave thing, you!)
- grass clippings from mowing the lawn
- birdseed (this one is great because what falls on the ground is later eaten by your locals).

Or get really madly messy and fill it with the guts of a pumpkin – this won't keep for more than one play, and it will require one hell of a clean-up, but goodness it is fun!
Don't forget to add tools for tipping and pouring and squishing and squashing. When you're done, either snap the lid on and store or get the hose out and give everyone and everything a quick once-over.

SLIME

SET-UP TIME   moderate
CLEAN-UP TIME   long
MESS FACTOR   high

Because this slime recipe uses only natural ingredients, it is unlikely to cause any skin irritations, but it *is* likely to have your child thinking, 'I wonder what would happen if I put my whole body into the slime?' The results are brilliant, but the clean-up is more than a quick wipe with a sponge. Be prepared for this to turn into a full-body experience. At the very least, have a clean towel ready; you will need it when they're done. The hose might come in handy, too. Don't say we didn't warn you!

YOU WILL NEED

a large bowl
food colouring
225ml (8 fl oz) warm water
250g (9 oz) cornflour
washing-up liquid (optional)
a whisk for mixing
a large tray or trough in
    which to play with the
    slime
spoons, whisks, funnels,
    sticks, hands …

In the bowl, mix the colour and the warm water, or, if using homemade colour, heat the food colouring without adding water. You can make the slime using cold water or cold food colouring, but the cornflour will be clumpier.

Slowly add the cornflour, mixing and blending as you go. If it's too runny, add more cornflour; if it's too firm, add more water. If you want the mixture to be a little more slippery, or you're hoping to give your patio or verandah a thorough clean when tidy-up time rolls around, then add in a little squirt of dishwashing liquid (too much will cut through the slimy qualities and leave you with a sloppy mess). You should be left with a substance that looks like a liquid but is firm to the touch.

Turn out your blob onto the tray or trough and let them at it. Drive toy cars through it, submerge animal figurines in it, mix it with sticks or attack it with cooking utensils.

This slime recipe looks far worse than it is. It dries hard and floury, so if they traipse it through the house, just wait for the mess to dry and vacuum it up. Outdoors, just set the hose on it – and your kids.

SIMPLE WATER PLAY

SET-UP TIME   short
CLEAN-UP TIME short
MESS FACTOR   moderate

There is nothing more straightforward and delightful than water play and, if you're not adding things like colour, glitter or mud, it can be one of the 'cleanest' messy plays around. Wet totally doesn't count as mess.

Obviously, as with all water play, your constant supervision is a must. It takes very little water to cause great harm. Besides, you won't want to miss a thing!

YOU WILL NEED

washing-up liquid or a gentle
    bubble bath
buckets, pots and pans
water
general kitchen implements
    that won't maim or injure

Squirt the washing-up liquid or bubble bath into the buckets, pots and pans. Provide a hose on low for the older children and let them enjoy filling their own vessels.

By all means crank out the colour, glitter and mud if you're happy to hose everything down afterwards – there is a certain charm to sparkly grass, after all. Funnels and spinning water wheels are always a hit and add an extra dimension to the play.

INDOOR ALTERNATIVE
Fill the kitchen sink with warm water, washing-up liquid and unbreakable dishes, or let them do the washing up with a part-filled bucket on a towel on the kitchen floor, so you can wash up together.

PAVEMENT PAINT

SET-UP TIME   *moderate*
CLEAN-UP TIME *moderate*
MESS FACTOR   *low*

This play is great fun from the start. Mixing is half the fun and painting the pavement opens up a whole new world of creative exploration. It washes off easily, so if the day is hot you can hose the kids and the art together for extra cleaning fun, or leave it and enjoy the new canvas until it rains.

YOU WILL NEED

125ml (4 fl oz) water
75g (2½ oz) cornflour
several different food
   colourings
muffin tin
paint brushes
a sunny day to enjoy

If you're using artificial colours, mix the water and cornflour and stir until it's well combined. You'll need to use some elbow grease. Put a couple of drops of colour in each compartment of the muffin tin. Pour the cornflour mix on top. Blend the mixture until the colour is well distributed.

If you're using natural colours, you won't need the water. Add equal parts food colouring and cornflour to each compartment of the muffin tin and blend well.

Get some paint brushes, find the kids a warm patch of pavement and enjoy some al fresco painting together.

MINIATURE PICNIC

SET-UP TIME   *moderate*
CLEAN-UP TIME *moderate*
MESS FACTOR   *moderate*

Why is it that things are so much more fun when miniaturised? Take a regular picnic and shrink it down for dolls and toys: perfect for an outing without leaving your property. You can make an outdoor fort using sheets, or just lay out a small blanket in a shady part of the garden.

YOU WILL NEED

sheets or a small picnic
    blanket
cushions
eggcups, jar lids, shells and
    other small containers
a selection of foods, all small
some interesting 'company' to
    share the picnic with

INDOOR ALTERNATIVE

Make an indoor picnic on the floor of the sitting room. Use sheets and the sofa to build a fort and pretend you're camping.

While you prepare the lunch selection, ask the kids to prepare the guests for a fine tea party. Get those teddies and dolls in their high-tea finest. Together you can set the scene with blankets and cushions. Welcome your guests to their big picnic date and enjoy a snack in the sunshine with some scintillating conversation.

Special doesn't always have to be cake and sweets. Toast cut into heart shapes using biscuit cutters and a cup of cool chamomile tea can make an average afternoon really special. Some great miniature picnic foods we have used are tiny carrot sticks, hummus served in eggcups, bean sprouts, pineapple squares, blueberries, strawberries, raisins, coconut flakes, watermelon cut into hearts with a biscuit cutter, and small pieces of banana, avocado and melon. Use jar lids, shells, seed pods or a child's tea set to serve the picnic.

ICE EXCAVATIONS

SET-UP TIME *long*
CLEAN-UP TIME *moderate*
MESS FACTOR *moderate*

The changing state of water from ice to evaporation is awe-inspiring science in its simplest form. By its very nature, ice is interesting to children. It's an open door for some cool learning and can be made into engaging play with very little effort. Get some motor skills in action, too, by becoming an ice-age archaeologist and excavating some frozen treasures with a wooden mallet or hammer or some cool water.

The possibilities with ice play are endless; the only thing that might hold you back is a little prep time needed the day before to allow enough time for your blocks to freeze.

YOU WILL NEED

food colouring
water
ice cube trays, muffin tins
  and/or zip-lock bags
interesting things to freeze
  (walnuts, small plastic toys,
  sticks)
tools to 'unlock' the trapped
  toys

The night before (or any time in advance if you want to have fun play ideas at the ready), mix the food colouring with water and distribute in the ice cube trays, muffin tins, zip-lock bags or similar vessels appropriate for the freezer. (Remember that water expands when frozen, which makes glass an unsafe option.)

Submerge toys, flowers or other interesting objects in what will become your ice blocks. Leave to freeze overnight.

When the sun comes out, bring out the jazzed-up ice and get the kids to attempt to free the treasures hidden inside by any means necessary. You can talk to them about how amazing it is that cold water melts ice like the hot sun does.

GARDEN SOUP

SET-UP TIME   *short*
CLEAN-UP TIME   *moderate–long*
MESS FACTOR   *high*

Warning: if you're particularly protective of your garden, this may not be the messy play for you. The 'garden soup' concept is simple and timeless: 'cooking' outdoors. The idea of mixing potions transcends generations, but be prepared: you will need to pretend to eat all manner of disgusting concoctions!

YOU WILL NEED

a bucket or other wide, water-holding container such as a small paddling pool or an old baby bath
water supply, such as a hose
mixing spoons
soil
some foliage to strip
cups to ladle the amazing brew into

Part-fill your container with water. Ask the children what kinds of ingredients they think will be needed to make garden soup.

Have the children add soil, leaves and flowers to the container and mix it up well. This is the soup! Ladle it out. Get them imagining and inventing and mixing and stirring. Make something revolting and messy and amazing. Embrace it, and marvel in the glory that is your offspring getting gunky, outdoorsy and adventurous.

Make a game of cleaning up by hosing down the play area (and muddy kids if the weather is warm enough!).

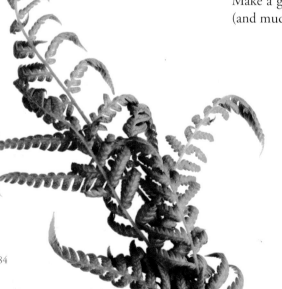

FIZZY ICE

SET-UP TIME   *long*
CLEAN-UP TIME *moderate*
MESS FACTOR   *moderate*

This play is a bit like fizz droppers in reverse and, because you're working with ice, it becomes an interesting outdoor play invitation. With changes in state, chemical reactions, temperature changes, colour and mess all meeting together, there is a lot here to be discovered and explored. Just think of it as a fun party bursting at the seams with people!

YOU WILL NEED

several different food
   colourings*
white vinegar
an ice cube tray
bicarbonate of soda
a tray or trough

Mix each food colour with some vinegar in the ice cube tray and freeze it.

When the vinegar ice has set, pop out the cubes and place them in the trough or tray outside. Let the children enjoy sprinkling bicarbonate of soda over the cubes, mixing them together, listening to the sound of the two reacting, watching the cubes turn brittle and foamy, then into colourful puddles, and making a big, fizzy rainbow soup.

When the little ones have finished, get the hose out and have fun washing away any spillages.

* Note: because you want to see a reaction between the vinegar and the bicarbonate of soda – and the more concentrated the vinegar is the better – in this instance, using concentrated shop-bought colour is advised as it won't dilute the vinegar like homemade colour will. Because it smells like vinegar does, children are unlikely to want to put it in their mouths anyway.

FAIRY HOUSING

SET-UP TIME   short
CLEAN-UP TIME short
MESS FACTOR   low

The truth is that fairies, just like everyone else, need somewhere to live. If you're finding your garden to be devoid of fairy inhabitants, it could be that you have not built them anywhere to live. Yet. Encourage enchantment, wonder and make-believe. Fairies are only unreal if you believe they are. Whimsy is something adults could all do with a little more of, and building a home for a fairy could be just the place to start.

YOU WILL NEED

twigs
leaves
soil
shells
flowers
imagination

Scope out the best real estate in your garden or patio. Keep in mind elements such as sunshine, shelter, views and access. In a pinch, fairies have been known to happily settle on a sunny window ledge or cosy fireplace mantlepiece, and plenty of urban fairies are quite at home tucked away in an attractive pot plant.

With your children, gather the materials you will need and construct your enchanted dwelling. Take your time and get creative with your construction. Play should be all about the process rather than the outcome.

You could use leaves for doors, twigs for fencing or walnut shells for outdoor seating. As long as it is fairy-sized, it is bound to appeal to any miniature-winged friend looking for a new abode. If your outdoors is not equipped with sufficient housing materials, you could construct a more modern abode with ice lolly sticks, toothpicks and cardboard. As long as it is biodegradable, it is okay by the fairies.

FACE PAINT

SET-UP TIME   moderate
CLEAN-UP TIME long
MESS FACTOR   high

As parents of small children, we spend an excessive amount of time wiping mess from clothes and faces. Why not simply embrace the chaos by opening a new world of artistic expression and play through self-face-painting? And, when they have exhausted the canvas of their own faces, reverse the roles and let the children paint you. Have them take control and marvel in the hilarity of everyone looking silly. Make sure you take lots of pictures, too.

This could just as easily be an indoor play activity but, just to be on the safe side, take it outdoors if you can. The less need to say 'no', the better for everyone.

YOU WILL NEED

plain moisturiser or body
   cream (not your finest eye
   serum)
an ice cube tray
a chopstick
cornflour
several different food
   colourings
paint brushes
a mirror

Put a little moisturiser into as many ice tray compartments as you are planning on colouring. Use the chopstick to mix in a little cornflour at a time. You want to thicken the mixture to a firm, paint-like consistency. If it's too runny, add more cornflour; if too lumpy, add more moisturiser.

Drop a different food colour into each compartment, remembering that natural colours require more, so you may need more cornflour to keep it paint-like.

Give the children brushes and a mirror, and let them go to town!

Artificial colours are more likely to leave a light stain on the skin, but it shouldn't be more than a little soap and warm water can handle.

BUCKET BATHS

SET-UP TIME *short*
CLEAN-UP TIME *moderate*
MESS FACTOR *low*

There is something endlessly amusing about your little ones fitting themselves into a small bucket of bubbly water. This play isn't just for summer, either: simply use warm water on a cold day. As the children get older, you can just sit beside them, participating without really doing anything other than enjoying the sunshine while they get busy. The less you have to do, the better!

Of course, with all bodies of water, as friendly as they may appear, you will need to watch your children closely at all times. Even a small amount of water can be fatal for young children without adequate supervision.

YOU WILL NEED

one bucket per child
bubble-bath mixture
water
toys (optional)
towels for after

Fill the buckets with water, adjusting the temperature to suit the day, and add bubbles. Put the buckets in the garden, on the deck or somewhere else outdoors and enjoy watching the children as they squeeze themselves into the buckets, spill all the water over the edge, transfer water from one bucket to another and take never-ending trips to the tap to refill the buckets again and again and again.

Add toys to turn a bucket into a car wash or a baby bath, or introduce an empty bucket and a cup and watch what happens.

BUBBLE BLOW DARTS

SET-UP TIME moderate (there is overnight preparation involved)
CLEAN-UP TIME short
MESS FACTOR low

Ah, the never-ending charm of bubbles: so shiny and attractive, like a less invasive form of glitter. Whether the appeal is the glistening rainbows captured inside the spheres or their fleeting delicacy, bubbles are enchanting and delightful no matter your age. Sure, for many younger children tipping bubble mixture over oneself is almost as good as making the actual bubbles, and learning how to blow bubbles is an art in itself, but making your own mixture means that not only is it lower in chemicals, but if the children end up wearing most of it you can always whip up some more.

YOU WILL NEED

a lidded container
225ml (8 fl oz) boiling water
2 tbsp sugar
2 tbsp washing-up liquid
straws
tape

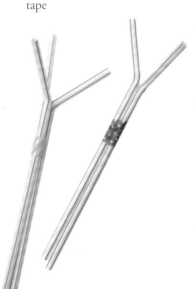

A lot of the success of the mixture is down to your personal environment – things like climate and brand of washing-up liquid can make a difference, so some tweaking of the recipe could be in order. You may need a little more dishwashing liquid, a little less sugar (too much will make the bubbles too heavy) or a little more time to infuse.

Add the boiling water and sugar to the container. When cool, gently add the dishwashing liquid – you don't want to agitate it so it gets foamy. Put the lid on the container and leave to stand overnight.

While you're waiting for your bubble mixture to infuse, you can ramp up the anticipation by creating the bubble dart blowers. Tape together three or four straws in a bundle to create one mega-straw. If your child is a little on the young side, you can still make a simple blow wand by fashioning one from a pipe cleaner.

The next fine day, get outdoors and start blowing. Enjoy the magic of watching small children trying to work out how to exhale on demand and catch something so fleeting in their hands.

BOAT RACING

SET-UP TIME *long*
CLEAN-UP TIME *short*
MESS FACTOR *low*

If it floats, it's a boat. But what kinds of boat are there? What moves quickly on water and what takes its time? Will a big stick move faster than a small one? Does the current of the water play some part in a vessel winning? So many questions! All can be answered by a little experimentation with a collection of boats and a moving body of water. Always be alert around water; supervise your chldren closely.

YOU WILL NEED

things that float (seed pods, leaves, walnut shells, dried avocado skins, half orange peels)
a moving body of water

Found items make the most interesting (and environmentally friendly) vessels. In fact, if you're sending any item down river, never to be seen again, it should only be made from natural matter. Besides, it is fun to make an activity of finding and collecting potential boats to store up for race day.

Have the children dress up their boats with leaves, mosses, shells and twigs. They can pick a side, choose their launching pad, wait for the right gust of wind, take their marks and GO! Repeat until they're all out of boats. And don't forget, next time you're out for a walk, to collect a boat or two for the next big race day.

TAKEAWAY PLAY

Children aren't always the most obliging travel, café or shopping companions. Actually, children are pretty disobliging in general. It's part of their job description. But, as adults, we can make the big overwhelming world a little more child-friendly by preparing for the worst-case scenario – because, let's face it, a colouring-in sheet and some scummy crayons aren't always that enticing to a kid.

All takeaway play involves some investment of time. But once you have a little kit of goodies, you can throw one in your handbag on your way out the door. What's more, these are all quiet and clean so you won't get kicked out of the café!

WALLET WONDERS

SET-UP TIME   short
CLEAN-UP TIME short
MESS FACTOR   low

There is a good chance you will forget to bring entertainment with you when heading out the door in a hurry; there is less chance of you forgetting your wallet. Thankfully, you can supercharge your wallet with tricks and treats to dole out when tempers veer towards the crabby end of the scale.

YOU WILL NEED

plasters
stickers
balloons
twist ties

All these things are small enough to fit in the change compartment of your wallet, and all have the potential to avoid a frustration meltdown. Supermarket trip about to turn pear-shaped? 'Let's see if you can be the doctor and put plasters on Mummy's hand!' Waiting to pick Gran up at the airport? Inflate a balloon and have an indoor game of ball. Stuck in a queue? Make spirals and chain links with twist-ties.

TIE IT UP

SET-UP TIME   *moderate*
CLEAN-UP TIME *short*
MESS FACTOR   *low*

The art of tying a lace can be, for the beginner, daunting and confusing. There are a dozen different ways to teach a child how to lace shoes, and most of them are frustrating when you're trying to get out of the door in a hurry. Practice can be fun and stress-free with a handbag-handy shoelace-board!

YOU WILL NEED

a piece of card
a hole punch
a shoelace
a marker or pen

On the piece of card, trace around a small child's shoe and mark out where you will punch your holes. The shoe does not have to be to scale. If you have a small handbag, by all means make a shoe card that fits in.

Punch two rows of three holes and lace up your 'shoe', ready for busy hands to practise on.

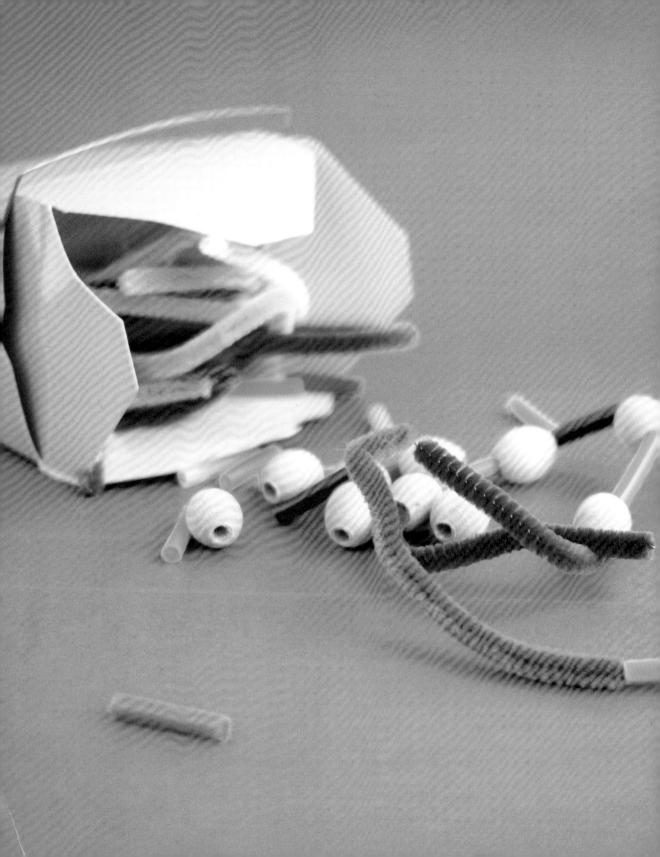

THREADING

SET-UP TIME   short
CLEAN-UP TIME short
MESS FACTOR   low

While threading is loads of fun at home, it is also a 'clean' messy play, as even if the beads go everywhere they are easy to scoop back up, and they leave no mark. Threading is also quiet, so it is great for takeaway play as there is no annoying beeping or buzzing to bother others. There may be sounds of joy and pride, though, and you may end up wearing some creative jewellery.

YOU WILL NEED

pipe cleaners
chunky beads
a small bag or box to contain
   them

Use the pipe cleaners as string and the beads to adorn them. Because the pipe cleaners are firm rather than flimsy, little hands are more capable of threading the beads onto them. It does require concentration and fine motor skills, and it can take a little while to master the art.

Your children may need to be prepared to share their supplies: adults seem to enjoy a little peaceful threading too.

STICKY NOTEBOOK

SET-UP TIME   *moderate*
CLEAN-UP TIME *short*
MESS FACTOR   *low*

This one is slightly different from the notebook you had that your kids made sticky with old food and grubby fingers! Paper and pencils are timeless and enduring. Choose coloured pencils over other drawing tools when out and about, because they are far less likely to transfer all over that lovely white tablecloth in the restaurant. They are also the easiest to do tricks with. Enter the self-adhesive Velcro!

YOU WILL NEED

self-adhesive Velcro dots or
    tape
scissors
a small notebook
pencils

On to the notebook cover, stick the soft loop side of the Velcro dots or tape cut to fit. Cut the hook side to fit the pencils and stick it on. Attach the pencils to the notebook.

Using the hook side on the pencils lets your kids experiment with sticking things to them if drawing is failing to ignite their interest.

RIBBON LEASH

SET-UP TIME   *short*
CLEAN-UP TIME   *short*
MESS FACTOR   *low*

This activity is so simple it is almost silly. When enduring babies' early experimentation with trajectory and gravity (and some days it really is a lesson in patience), a length of ribbon can be your saving grace, expecially when you find yourself in a small, confined space.

YOU WILL NEED

a length or two of ribbon
favourite or new toys

Attaching the toy of the moment to a ribbon leash will make retrieving the object a breeze when your cherub attempts to make it fly. No more scrambling down aeroplane aisles; just reel it in like you landed the big one. 'You throw that zebra as much as you like, sweet pea!'

POMPOM PUSHERS

SET-UP TIME   *moderate*
CLEAN-UP TIME *short*
MESS FACTOR   *low*

Sometimes the silence of concentration comes from the simplest of play. As with all takeaway play, this is clean and quiet and can appeal to a wide age range of pre-schoolers.

YOU WILL NEED

a small disposable plastic
    container with a lid
a craft knife
a handful of pompoms of
    different colours

Cut a hole in the lid of the container just big enough to push a pompom through. Fill the container with the pompoms and put the lid on. Providing the hole you have cut is not too big, the pompoms shouldn't escape to roll around in the bottom of your handbag.

When you're out and about, remove the pompoms and ask your child to put them back into the container one at a time through the hole. It might sound like a mundane task, but it really is engaging. The next time, see if she can put in just the blue pompoms, then just the yellow ones!

PHOTO BOOK

SET-UP TIME   *moderate*
CLEAN-UP TIME *short*
MESS FACTOR   *low*

Children are naturally attracted to other children and they love people's faces and expressions. A small photo book with family snaps can keep a toddler going when story books fail, because nothing is more interesting than you!

YOU WILL NEED

pictures – either family
   photos or magazine
   cuttings
scissors
a small photo album or
   notebook
glue

Option 1: Family Album

Select your family snaps. This alone can be fun to do together for the nostalgia and story-telling opportunities. It is lovely for young children to hear stories such as the time Mum and Dad took a picnic before there were babies involved, or to see photos of Daddy as a little boy.

Fill up the photo album and, next time you're on the train, pull it out and tell a few more stories. What was that dog's name again? What was that funny thing it used to do? It is all gold.

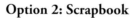

Option 2: Scrapbook

Select some age-appropriate photos from magazines together and enjoy a little scrapbooking in the notebook. Your children will love revisiting the images and making up stories from them.

MEASUREMENTS

SET-UP TIME   *short*
CLEAN-UP TIME *short*
MESS FACTOR   *low*

Height, weight, length and temperature are all fascinating but confusing concepts. The simple idea of quantifying anything is actually pretty cool in itself, and instilling the idea that mathematics is amazing starts at the very beginning. Children don't need to have a sound understanding of numbers to enjoy the concept. As long as it's presented in a fun way, they will keep on enjoying it. 'Tenner-two-foursey' is totally a legitimate measurement.

YOU WILL NEED

a measuring tape, either
    child-friendly retractable or
    a soft tailor's tape or a ruler
a notebook (the sticky
    notebook from page 109 is
    ideal)
items to measure

No matter where you are, there will always be something to quantify. If you can't measure it, then perhaps you can run a poll or do some statistical analysis:

'How many yellow cars can you spot when we drive to Nana's place?'

'Can you count the number of dogs we see when we walk home?'

'Is the length of your teaspoon different from the length of Mum's?'

'How high is your seat?'

The questions and answers are endless.

CARD GAMES

SET-UP TIME *moderate*
CLEAN-UP TIME *short*
MESS FACTOR *low*

Are you playing with less than a full deck? If your children have found your playing cards, chances are they've given them the special treatment, and you may be wondering what to do with the cards that remain. Cut your losses and up-cycle them into some fun takeaway play.

YOU WILL NEED

textures (fabrics, trims,
  ribbons, buttons)
scissors
decent grown-ups' glue
playing cards (or raid that
  stash of business cards from
  people you're never going to
  get in touch with)

Cut and collate matching pairs of interesting textures, such as two identical lengths of ribbon, two strips of the same fabric, two interesting buttons or two curious trims. Enjoy an evening of adhesion, gluing your collection to the cards (one piece per card) and allowing them to dry before tucking them into a snap-lock bag for later use.

When you're out and about, enjoy watching your children match them up, play memory or just marvel in the sensory experience of touchy-feely cards.

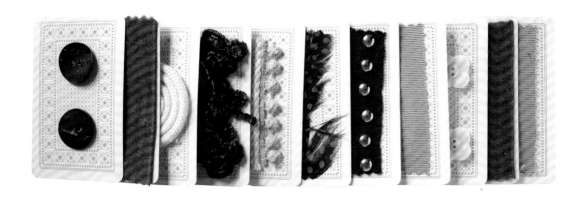

COIN COUNTERS

SET-UP TIME   *short*
CLEAN-UP TIME *short*
MESS FACTOR   *low*

Waiting for a meal at a restaurant? Got a stash of coins in your wallet? Not sure how many there are? Get the kids to count them out for you! Kids can't count yet? This matching game makes it easy for those who haven't yet figured out numeracy.

YOU WILL NEED

thin card or paper
scissors
a soft pencil (e.g. 2B–3B)
coins (one of each of your
   currency)

Cut the card or paper into a credit-card size (this way it will slip easily into your wallet). Then either trace around your coins one at a time and write the denominations inside, or create a rubbing of each coin by placing it head-side up under the card or paper and rubbing the pencil over the grooves and indents. The face of the currency should appear in a perfect likeness.

Tip out the contents of your coin purse and ask your child to match each coin to its image.

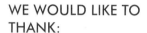

ACKNOWLEDGEMENTS

WE WOULD LIKE TO THANK:

Marilyn Biderman, in our corner from the beginning.

Our supplies, props and locations were loaned to us by some amazing people and businesses. Thank you Oceania Imports for providing all the buttons and trims, Saben for the luxe wallet, Superette for the jewellery, Heirloom Designs for the cushion, the Russell family home, the Crow family home, Dizengoff, Rabbit Hole and Richmond Road Café.

To our incredible team at Penguin New Zealand: Katie Haworth, Tessa King and Lucy Hutchings. What a dream team. Lucky were we to have you behind us. Your guidance and support put the glitter on top.

Thank you to our models, Margaux and Frankie McElhinney, Roman and Zana Crow,

Hannah Godfrey, Andrew Mitchener, Evie and Esther Probert, Kate, Tom and Meg Edinborough, Michaela Clark. Mez and Rico, your generosity overwhelms.

All our love to our amazing and supportive family, and their families. All our sisters, their partners and children. Bonnie, James, Roman, Zana, Lili, Amelia, Andrew. In-laws, grandparents, and the family who live in our hearts.

And to our parents, who gave us such rich childhood play experiences to draw from. The original proponent of free play had to be you, Mama. Your relentless support, encouragement, time, compassion and love is never lost on us. There are not enough thanks to sufficiently convey the depth of our appreciation and love for you.

RACHEL WOULD LIKE TO THANK:

Thank you to my girls. You have been the most willing of test subjects, and suffered through many a failed recipe (I will never mention the spirulina playdough incident again, but the smell lingers on). Your enthusiasm to experiment makes it easy to keep coming up with new ideas.

Bonnie Sumner, thank you for your fresh and critical eyes; your opinion and expertise is always my first port of call in matters of words. Forever my first editor.

Sarah Byers, Kate Bradway, and Niqi Ogletree, always the first off the block to offer help and support.

To Renwick Playcentre, and Wendy Rogerson, you showed me that messy play is not to be feared. You held my hand and

walked me to the light of free and unstructured play. I may not have embraced glitter, but everything else I learned from you.

The work of New Zealand Early Childhood Education framework Te Whaariki, the incredible Pennie Brownlee and Alfie Kohn were instrumental in opening my eyes to play free from outcomes, to the value of the child-led experience.

Appreciation for my online bints. Ever-willing test subjects and feedback providers, never mind keeping me sane when everything gets a little too rock and roll. I much prefer country.

And lastly to my sister Ruth, thank you! You manage to turn a vague waffly thought into a clear and beautiful reality. None of this is possible without you. Your talent and skill never cease to astound me.

RUTH WOULD LIKE TO THANK:

The look of this book owes a great debt to many people.

I can't imagine better guides to the world of messy play than my nephew Roman and my nieces Margaux, Frankie and Zana. You are all the best of teachers, models and companions.

Special thanks goes to Andrew, to whom I owe this book, no printed matter can ever convey my love for you.

In Rachel Sumner I have everything a sister could ask for in a colleague: inspiration, encouragement, honesty, patience and friendship. An overflowing basket full of thanks goes to my big sister Bonnie, for keeping me well fuelled with amazing raw vegan treats and for her constant

support and inspiration. I am eternally thankful to my father Bruce White, for initially instilling the passion for photography in me from those very early years in the darkroom. I am also greatly indebted to my Pappy, Thomas Burstyn for generously giving his time and considerable skills and for so much valued photography advice.

I also want to thank Jude Mitchener for allowing me to destroy her house on photoshoots; James Crow for his constant enthusiasm; Bettina Neu for believing in me from the start; Simon Fraser for your constant support; Tim Miller for your wisdom and zest; and of course I want to thank Pinterest for always being there for me.

AUTHOR BIOGRAPHIES

Writer Rachel Sumner and designer Ruth Mitchener are sisters. They have very different skills but share their interests in children and communication. Their creative process is very collaborative, and they share a passion for excellence in content and detail. Sometimes Rachel gets a bit bossy because she is older, but Ruth is normally right.

ABOUT RACHEL

Writer Rachel Sumner is a prolific blogger and book addict. She lives in Auckland with her two wonderful girls and a ginger cat called Ginger.

Prior to having children Rachel was the children's book sales rep for independent retailer Beattie And Forbes Booksellers working with schools and libraries across Hawkes Bay.

She spent 12 months as the children's book reviewer for the *Marlborough Express* in Blenheim and is currently a book reviewer for *The Australian Women's Weekly*.

ABOUT RUTH

Ruth Mitchener (née Sumner) is a multi-award winning designer, who lives in Auckland, New Zealand.

After studying Fine Arts in a decommissioned monastery, filling countless sketchbooks on a 9-month sabbatical in Europe, manufacturing medicines at Weleda, and starting her own designer cushion business, Ruth went on to complete a degree in Industrial Design at Victoria University of Wellington with first class honours.

She is passionate about creating clean, beautiful and intriguing imagery that not only accurately reflects the written word but translates those words into memorable and intriguing images.

INDEX